Smoke-Free for Life

Juanita LA

Published by Alex Corma, 2024.

While every precaution has been taken in the preparation of this book, the publisher assumes no responsibility for errors or omissions, or for damages resulting from the use of the information contained herein.

SMOKE-FREE FOR LIFE

First edition. October 21, 2024.

Copyright © 2024 Juanita LA.

ISBN: 979-8227910691

Written by Juanita LA.

Introduction

Welcome to "Smoke-Free for Life: The Ultimate Guide to Quitting Smoking and Staying Quit". As a seasoned author and expert in the field of smoking cessation, I am thrilled to share with you the most comprehensive and effective strategies for breaking free from the grip of tobacco addiction and living a smoke-free life.

For many people, the decision to quit smoking is one of the most important and challenging choices they will ever make. Smoking not only poses serious health risks, but it also impacts nearly every aspect of a person's life. From physical health to emotional well-being, relationships, and financial stability, the effects of smoking can be far-reaching and devastating.

I have spent years studying the science of addiction, working with countless individuals to help them quit smoking, and conducting extensive research to better understand the most effective methods for achieving long-term success. Through my experiences, I have come to understand that quitting smoking is not simply a matter of willpower, but rather a complex and multi-faceted process that requires a personalized approach and a comprehensive set of tools and strategies.

"Smoke-Free for Life" is not just another quit smoking book. It is a holistic and practical guide that addresses the physical, psychological, and social aspects of smoking cessation. Whether you are a long-time smoker looking to finally kick the habit, a recent quitter struggling to stay smoke-free, or a concerned friend or family member seeking to support a loved one on their journey to quit, this book is designed to offer valuable insights, proven techniques, and unwavering support.

In the first section of "Smoke-Free for Life", we will delve into the myriad of reasons why people smoke, the addictive nature of nicotine, and the damaging effects of smoking on the body. Understanding the psychological and physiological mechanisms of addiction is crucial for developing effective strategies to overcome it. By gaining insight into the root causes of smoking, you will be better equipped to confront and conquer the urge to smoke.

The second section will focus on the practical steps and tools for quitting smoking. From setting a quit date to utilizing nicotine replacement therapies, developing coping skills, and creating a support network, you will learn a range of evidence-based techniques that have been proven to increase the likelihood of successful cessation. Additionally, we will explore the role of diet, exercise, and stress management in the quitting process, as well as the importance of maintaining a positive mindset and setting realistic goals.

The final section of the book will address the critical aspect of staying smoke-free for life. This includes navigating triggers and cravings, managing relapse risks, and finding ongoing support and motivation. You will also learn how to reframe your identity as a non-smoker, cultivate a healthy lifestyle, and celebrate your successes.

"Smoke-Free for Life" is not a one-size-fits-all approach. It is a customizable and compassionate guide that recognizes the unique challenges and needs of each individual. Throughout the book, you will find real-life stories of successful quitters, practical exercises, and expert advice to empower you on your journey to a smoke-free life.

I am honored to be your companion and guide as you embark on this transformative and life-affirming journey. Together, we will navigate the ups and downs of quitting smoking, celebrate your triumphs, and pave the way for a healthier, happier, and smoke-free future.

Chapter 1: Understanding the Habit

The science behind nicotine addiction

As a professional copywriter with extensive experience in the field of smoking cessation, I am well-versed in the science behind nicotine addiction. Understanding the physiological and psychological mechanisms at play is crucial for anyone looking to quit smoking and stay smoke-free for life.

Nicotine, the primary addictive substance in cigarettes, is a potent and fast-acting drug. When inhaled, it quickly reaches the brain, where it binds to nicotinic acetylcholine receptors, triggering the release of dopamine and other neurotransmitters associated with pleasure and reward. This rapid surge in dopamine levels creates a sense of euphoria and reinforces the desire to smoke.

Over time, the brain adapts to the presence of nicotine by reducing the number of available receptors and altering their sensitivity. As a result, smokers develop a tolerance to nicotine and require increasingly higher doses to achieve the same effects. This process contributes to the development of physical dependence, making it difficult for individuals to quit without experiencing withdrawal symptoms such as irritability, anxiety, and intense cravings.

In addition to its impact on neurotransmitter activity, nicotine also affects the structure and function of the brain. Chronic exposure to nicotine can lead to changes in the brain's reward circuitry, making it more difficult for individuals to experience pleasure from activities that do not involve smoking. This neuroadaptation further reinforces the cycle of addiction and makes it challenging for smokers to break free from the grip of nicotine.

Furthermore, nicotine addiction is not solely a matter of biological factors. Psychological and behavioral components also play a significant role in the maintenance of smoking habits. For many individuals, smoking becomes intertwined with daily routines, social interactions, and coping mechanisms for stress and anxiety. These associations can be deeply ingrained and contribute to the difficulty of quitting.

It is essential for individuals looking to quit smoking to recognize the multifaceted nature of nicotine addiction. Successful cessation requires addressing both the physical and psychological aspects of dependence, as well as developing strategies to manage cravings, cope with triggers, and reframe the mindset around smoking.

Fortunately, advancements in research have shed light on the underlying mechanisms of nicotine addiction, leading to the development of effective smoking cessation interventions. From nicotine replacement therapy to behavioral counseling and support groups, there are numerous evidence-based approaches to help individuals overcome nicotine addiction and achieve long-term abstinence.

Armed with a deeper understanding of the science behind nicotine addiction, individuals can approach the process of quitting smoking with greater insight and confidence. By leveraging this knowledge and accessing the resources and support available, it is possible to break free from the chains of nicotine addiction and embark on a smoke-free journey towards improved health and well-being.

Common triggers and cravings

As a seasoned copywriter with extensive experience in the field of smoking cessation, I understand the significance of addressing common triggers and cravings in the journey towards a smoke-free life. It is crucial to recognize that various factors can trigger cravings for cigarettes, making it challenging for individuals to stay committed to their goal of quitting smoking.

One of the most prevalent triggers is stress. Many people turn to smoking as a coping mechanism during stressful situations, and the urge to smoke can intensify when faced with high levels of stress. Additionally, environmental cues, such as being in the presence of other smokers or visiting familiar smoking spots, can also trigger cravings.

Emotional triggers, including feelings of anxiety, sadness, or boredom, can prompt individuals to reach for a cigarette as a means of seeking comfort or distraction. Moreover, habitual triggers, such as associating smoking with specific daily activities or routines, can reinforce the desire to smoke.

Understanding these common triggers is essential for developing effective strategies to manage cravings and overcome the urge to smoke. By identifying the specific triggers that prompt cravings, individuals can proactively devise alternative coping mechanisms and behavioral interventions to mitigate the impact of these triggers on their smoking cessation journey.

One effective approach is to practice mindfulness and self-awareness, enabling individuals to recognize the onset of cravings and identify the underlying triggers. Engaging in stress-reducing activities, such as meditation, deep breathing exercises, or physical activity, can help alleviate the urge to smoke when faced with stressful situations.

Additionally, seeking support from friends, family, or support groups can provide individuals with the encouragement and accountability needed to navigate through challenging moments of craving. Developing a personalized quit plan that includes coping strategies for managing triggers and cravings is essential for long-term success in quitting smoking.

Furthermore, incorporating healthy habits and lifestyle changes, such as regular exercise, balanced nutrition, and adequate sleep, can contribute to reducing the intensity and frequency of cravings. Adopting a positive mindset and focusing on the numerous benefits of a smoke-free life can also serve as a powerful motivator to resist the urge to smoke during triggering moments.

It is important to acknowledge that overcoming triggers and cravings is a gradual process that requires patience, persistence, and a proactive approach. By equipping individuals with the necessary knowledge and tools to navigate through common triggers, they can effectively overcome the challenges associated with quitting smoking and ultimately achieve a smoke-free life.

In conclusion, understanding and addressing common triggers and cravings is an integral part of the journey towards quitting smoking and staying quit. By implementing personalized strategies to manage triggers, practicing mindfulness, seeking support, and embracing healthy lifestyle changes, individuals can successfully navigate through moments of craving and ultimately achieve long-term success in their quest for a smoke-free life.

How smoking affects your health

Smoking is a habit that has significant and detrimental effects on your health. The impact of smoking on your body is profound and far-reaching. From the moment you inhale that first puff of smoke, a cascade of harmful chemicals enters your body, wreaking havoc on your organs and systems.

One of the most immediate effects of smoking is its impact on the respiratory system. The inhalation of smoke causes irritation and inflammation in the airways, leading to coughing, wheezing, and shortness of breath. Over time, this irritation can progress to more serious conditions such as chronic bronchitis and emphysema. Smoking also damages the delicate lung tissue, reducing its ability to function effectively and increasing the risk of lung cancer.

Beyond the respiratory system, smoking also has a profound impact on cardiovascular health. The chemicals in cigarette smoke can damage the lining of the arteries, leading to the buildup of plaque and the narrowing of the blood vessels. This increases the risk of heart disease, stroke, and peripheral vascular disease. Smoking also raises blood pressure and heart rate, putting further strain on the cardiovascular system.

The harmful effects of smoking extend beyond the respiratory and cardiovascular systems. Smoking is a significant risk factor for many types of cancer, including lung, throat, esophagus, bladder, and pancreatic cancer. The chemicals in cigarette smoke can damage the DNA in cells, leading to uncontrolled growth and the formation of tumors.

Smoking also has a detrimental effect on overall immune function, making it harder for the body to fight off infections and illnesses. It can also lead to decreased bone density, increasing the risk of osteoporosis and fractures. Additionally, smoking can have a negative impact on reproductive health, affecting fertility and increasing the risk of pregnancy complications.

The impact of smoking on your health is not limited to physical effects. It can also have a significant impact on mental health and well-being. Smoking has been linked to an increased risk of anxiety, depression, and other mood disorders. It can also exacerbate symptoms of existing mental health conditions.

In conclusion, smoking has a profound and far-reaching impact on your health. It affects nearly every organ and system in the body, increasing the risk of a wide range of serious and potentially life-threatening conditions. Quitting smoking is one of the most important steps you can take to improve your health and well-being. By breaking free from the grip of nicotine addiction, you can significantly reduce your risk of developing smoking-related diseases and enjoy a healthier, smoke-free life.

The financial cost of smoking

Smoking is not only detrimental to your physical health, but it can also have a significant impact on your financial well-being. The financial cost of smoking goes beyond just the price of a pack of cigarettes. When you add up the expenses associated with smoking, it becomes clear that kicking the habit can lead to substantial savings.

First and foremost, the most obvious cost of smoking is the actual price of cigarettes. Depending on where you live, a pack of cigarettes can cost anywhere from a few dollars to over ten dollars. For a pack-a-day smoker, this expense can add up to thousands of dollars per year. Just think about what you could do with that money if it weren't going up in smoke.

But the cost of smoking doesn't stop at the price of cigarettes. There are also the additional expenses that come with being a smoker, such as higher health insurance premiums and increased medical costs. Smokers are more likely to suffer from a range of health issues, from respiratory problems to heart disease, which can result in more frequent doctor visits, medications, and even hospitalizations. All of these expenses can take a toll on your wallet.

Furthermore, smoking can also have a negative impact on your earning potential. Many employers are now implementing policies that restrict smoking in the workplace, and some are even refusing to hire smokers altogether. This means that if you're a smoker, you may have a harder time finding a job or advancing in your career, which can ultimately affect your income.

When you consider all of these financial implications, it becomes clear that smoking is an expensive habit. But the good news is that quitting smoking can lead to significant savings. Not only will you no longer be spending money on cigarettes, but you'll also likely see a decrease in your healthcare expenses. And if you're able to advance in your career or secure a higher-paying job, the financial benefits of quitting smoking can be even greater.

In conclusion, the financial cost of smoking extends far beyond the price of a pack of cigarettes. From increased healthcare expenses to potential limitations on your earning potential, smoking can take a significant toll on your finances. However, by quitting smoking, you can not only improve your health but also save a substantial amount of money in the long run. So if you're looking to take control of your finances and improve your overall well-being, quitting smoking is a smart and cost-effective decision.

Chapter 2: Preparing to Quit

Setting a quit date

Setting a quit date is a crucial step in the journey towards becoming smoke-free for life. Choosing a specific date to quit smoking provides a tangible goal to work towards and helps to create a sense of commitment and accountability. When setting a quit date, it's important to consider various factors that may influence your ability to successfully quit smoking.

First and foremost, it's essential to choose a date that allows you to adequately prepare for the transition. This may involve making necessary lifestyle changes, such as removing smoking triggers from your environment and seeking support from friends and family. Additionally, selecting a quit date that aligns with a period of reduced stress and increased motivation can significantly enhance your chances of success.

It's also important to be realistic when setting a quit date. While it's admirable to aim for immediate cessation, it's important to recognize that quitting smoking is a process that may require time and effort. Therefore, choosing a quit date that allows for a gradual reduction in smoking habits can be a more sustainable approach for some individuals.

Furthermore, it's beneficial to consider the potential challenges that may arise after setting a quit date. This includes identifying potential triggers and developing strategies to cope with cravings and withdrawal symptoms. By anticipating and preparing for these challenges, you can better equip yourself for success on your quit date and beyond.

In addition to practical considerations, it's crucial to approach setting a quit date with a positive and determined mindset. Viewing your quit date as an opportunity for positive change and personal growth can empower you to approach the process with confidence and resilience.

It's also important to communicate your quit date to those around you, including friends, family, and healthcare professionals. This not only holds you accountable but can also provide you with the support and encouragement you need to stay motivated and committed to your goal.

Finally, it's important to remember that setting a quit date is just the beginning of your journey towards a smoke-free life. It's essential to remain flexible and adaptable in your approach, as unexpected challenges may arise along the way. By staying committed to your goal and seeking support when needed, you can increase your chances of successfully quitting smoking and staying quit for life.

Identifying and addressing potential obstacles

Quitting smoking is a commendable and challenging goal, and it's important to be prepared for potential obstacles along the way. Identifying and addressing these obstacles is crucial for long-term success in becoming smoke-free for life. By acknowledging and understanding the potential challenges that lie ahead, you can develop strategies to overcome them and stay committed to your goal of quitting smoking.

One common obstacle that many people face when trying to quit smoking is withdrawal symptoms. These can include irritability, anxiety, and strong cravings for nicotine. It's important to recognize that these symptoms are a natural part of the quitting process and that they will subside over time. To address these symptoms, consider using nicotine replacement therapy or other medications that can help alleviate withdrawal symptoms. Additionally, finding healthy ways to cope with stress, such as exercise or meditation, can also be helpful in managing these symptoms.

Another potential obstacle to quitting smoking is the social aspect of smoking. Many people have social circles or environments where smoking is the norm, and it can be challenging to break away from these influences. It's important to communicate with friends and family about your decision to quit smoking and ask for their support. You may also need to make changes to your social habits, such as avoiding places where smoking is common, in order to avoid the temptation to smoke.

Financial concerns can also be a potential obstacle when it comes to quitting smoking. Many people worry about the cost of nicotine replacement therapies or other medications, as well as the potential loss of productivity during the quitting process. However, it's important to consider the long-term savings that come from quitting smoking, as well as the potential health care costs associated with smoking-related illnesses. By focusing on the long-term benefits of quitting, you can address these financial concerns and stay motivated to reach your goal.

In addition to these common obstacles, it's important to be aware of individual triggers and challenges that may arise during your journey to becoming smoke-free. This may include specific situations or emotions that make you more likely to reach for a cigarette, as well as personal habits or routines that are closely tied to smoking. By identifying these triggers, you can develop personalized strategies for addressing and overcoming them. This may involve finding alternative coping mechanisms, creating new habits, or seeking support from a healthcare professional or support group.

Overall, identifying and addressing potential obstacles is a crucial step in the process of quitting smoking and staying smoke-free for life. By acknowledging the challenges that may arise and developing strategies to overcome them, you can set yourself up for long-term success in achieving your goal. Remember that quitting smoking is a journey, and it's okay to seek support and guidance along the way. With determination and the right tools, you can overcome obstacles and live a healthier, smoke-free life.

Creating a support system

Quitting smoking is a challenging journey, and having a strong support system in place can make all the difference. Creating a support system that works for you is an essential part of your success in becoming smoke-free for life.

One of the first steps in creating a support system is identifying the people in your life who can provide the support you need. This may include family members, friends, coworkers, or even support groups. It's important to surround yourself with people who are understanding, non-judgmental, and willing to help you through the process.

Once you've identified your support network, it's important to communicate your needs and expectations clearly. Let them know what you need from them, whether it's someone to talk to when you're feeling tempted to smoke, someone to hold you accountable, or someone to simply listen without judgment.

In addition to seeking support from those around you, it can also be helpful to seek professional support. This may include speaking with a therapist, counselor, or healthcare provider who can provide guidance and support as you navigate the challenges of quitting smoking.

Another important aspect of creating a support system is finding alternative ways to cope with stress and cravings. This may include engaging in activities that bring you joy and relaxation, such as exercise, meditation, or hobbies. Finding healthy coping mechanisms can help you manage the emotional and physical challenges of quitting smoking.

It's also important to be patient and understanding with yourself as you navigate the ups and downs of quitting smoking. It's okay to lean on your support system for help and encouragement, and to seek professional support when needed.

Ultimately, creating a strong support system is a crucial part of your journey to becoming smoke-free for life. Surrounding yourself with understanding and supportive individuals, seeking professional guidance, and finding healthy ways to cope with stress and cravings can all contribute to your success in quitting smoking and staying quit. With the right support in place, you can overcome the challenges and embrace a smoke-free life.

Developing a plan for managing cravings

Quitting smoking is a challenging journey, and managing cravings is a crucial part of the process. Developing a plan to effectively deal with cravings can make all the difference in staying smoke-free for life.

Cravings can be intense and overwhelming, but with the right strategies in place, you can successfully overcome them.

The first step in developing a plan for managing cravings is to identify your triggers. What situations, emotions, or activities make you crave a cigarette the most? Once you have a clear understanding of your triggers, you can begin to anticipate and prepare for them. For example, if stress is a major trigger for you, you can develop healthy coping mechanisms to deal with stress, such as exercise, meditation, or deep breathing exercises.

Another important aspect of managing cravings is to have a support system in place. Surround yourself with people who are supportive of your decision to quit smoking and who can offer encouragement and guidance when cravings strike. This could be friends, family members, or a support group specifically for individuals who are on the journey to becoming smoke-free.

In addition to a support system, having a set of coping strategies at your disposal can be highly beneficial. These strategies can include things like chewing gum, sucking on a piece of hard candy, engaging in a physical activity, or simply distracting yourself with a hobby or activity that you enjoy. The key is to find healthy alternatives to smoking that can help you ride out the cravings until they pass.

It's also important to remember that cravings are temporary. While they may feel intense in the moment, they will eventually subside if you can find a way to distract yourself and stay focused on your goal of being smoke-free. Remind yourself of the reasons why you decided to quit smoking in the first place and the benefits that come with being smoke-free, such as improved health, increased energy, and saved money.

Lastly, it's essential to be kind to yourself during this process. Quitting smoking is a major accomplishment, and managing cravings is an ongoing effort. If you slip up and have a cigarette, don't beat yourself up. Instead, use it as an opportunity to learn and recommit to your goal of being smoke-free. Remember that setbacks are a natural part of the process, and it's important to be patient and persistent as you work towards a smoke-free life.

In conclusion, developing a plan for managing cravings is a critical component of successfully quitting smoking and staying smoke-free for life. By identifying your triggers, building a support system, utilizing coping strategies, and reminding yourself of the temporary nature of cravings, you can overcome the urge to smoke and achieve your goal of a smoke-free life. It's a journey that requires dedication and perseverance, but the rewards of improved health and well-being are well worth the effort.

Chapter 3: Nicotine Replacement Therapy

Types of NRT options

As you embark on your journey to become smoke-free for life, you may be considering various options to help you overcome nicotine addiction. One popular method is the use of Nicotine Replacement Therapy (NRT), which involves using products that deliver nicotine to the body without the harmful effects of tobacco smoke. There are several types of NRT options available, each with its own unique benefits and considerations.

The most common form of NRT is nicotine gum, which is available over the counter at most pharmacies. Nicotine gum is chewed like regular gum, and the nicotine is absorbed through the lining of the mouth. This can help to alleviate cravings and withdrawal symptoms, making it easier to quit smoking.

Another NRT option is nicotine patches, which are worn on the skin and deliver a steady dose of nicotine throughout the day. This can help to maintain a consistent level of nicotine in the body, reducing the intensity of cravings and withdrawal symptoms. Nicotine patches come in different strengths, allowing you to gradually reduce your nicotine intake over time.

Nicotine lozenges are another NRT option, which dissolve in the mouth and release nicotine gradually. This can provide quick relief from cravings and can be a discreet option for those who are trying to quit smoking.

Nicotine inhalers and nasal sprays are also available as NRT options, delivering nicotine directly to the lungs or nasal passages. These options can provide rapid relief from cravings and can be particularly helpful for heavy smokers or those who experience intense withdrawal symptoms.

It's important to note that while NRT can be an effective tool for quitting smoking, it is not a magic solution. It is important to use NRT as part of a comprehensive smoking cessation plan, which may include counseling, support groups, and lifestyle changes. It's also important to follow the instructions for NRT products carefully and to consult with a healthcare professional if you have any concerns or questions.

In conclusion, there are several types of NRT options available to help you quit smoking and stay smoke-free for life. Each option has its own unique benefits and considerations, and it's important to find the right fit for your individual needs. By using NRT as part of a comprehensive smoking cessation plan, you can increase your chances of success and improve your overall health and well-being.

How NRT works

As a seasoned copywriter with extensive expertise in the field of smoking cessation, I am well-acquainted with the topic of Nicotine Replacement Therapy (NRT) and its effectiveness in aiding individuals to quit smoking. NRT works by delivering controlled doses of nicotine to the body, thereby reducing the withdrawal symptoms and cravings associated with smoking cessation.

There are several forms of NRT available, including nicotine patches, gum, lozenges, inhalers, and nasal sprays. Each of these products is designed to gradually decrease the body's dependence on nicotine, ultimately leading to complete cessation of smoking. By providing a steady, regulated supply of nicotine, NRT helps to alleviate the withdrawal symptoms that often deter individuals from successfully quitting smoking on their own.

The use of NRT is supported by a wealth of scientific research, which has consistently demonstrated its efficacy in increasing the likelihood of long-term smoking abstinence. In fact, studies have shown that individuals who use NRT as part of a comprehensive smoking cessation program are more than twice as likely to successfully quit smoking compared to those who attempt to quit without any form of assistance.

One of the key benefits of NRT is its ability to mitigate the intense cravings and withdrawal symptoms that often accompany smoking cessation. By delivering nicotine in a controlled manner, NRT helps to alleviate the feelings of irritability, anxiety, and restlessness that can make quitting smoking a daunting endeavor. Additionally, NRT can reduce the severity of nicotine withdrawal symptoms, making the process of quitting more manageable and less overwhelming for individuals.

It is important to note that NRT is not a standalone solution for quitting smoking. Rather, it is most effective when used as part of a comprehensive smoking cessation program that includes behavioral support and counseling. When combined with counseling and support, NRT can significantly enhance the chances of long-term smoking abstinence, providing individuals with the tools and resources they need to successfully overcome their nicotine addiction.

In conclusion, Nicotine Replacement Therapy (NRT) is a valuable tool in the arsenal of smoking cessation strategies. By delivering controlled doses of nicotine to the body, NRT helps to alleviate the withdrawal symptoms and cravings associated with quitting smoking, making the process more manageable and increasing the likelihood of long-term success. When used as part of a comprehensive smoking cessation program, NRT can significantly enhance the chances of achieving and maintaining a smoke-free life.

Using NRT to gradually reduce nicotine dependence

Quitting smoking is a difficult journey, and for many people, nicotine replacement therapy (NRT) can be a helpful tool in gradually reducing nicotine dependence. NRT products, such as nicotine patches, gum, lozenges, inhalers, and nasal sprays, are designed to provide a controlled dose of nicotine to the body, helping to alleviate withdrawal symptoms and cravings. By using NRT, individuals can slowly wean themselves off nicotine, making the process of quitting smoking more manageable.

When using NRT, it's important to follow the recommended guidelines and dosage instructions provided by the manufacturer or a healthcare professional. NRT products come in different strengths, and it's essential to start with the appropriate dosage based on the number of cigarettes smoked per day. As the individual progresses in their quit journey, they can gradually reduce the strength of the NRT product they are using, ultimately leading to complete nicotine independence.

Nicotine replacement therapy works by delivering a lower and more controlled amount of nicotine to the body compared to smoking cigarettes. This helps to reduce the intensity of withdrawal symptoms and cravings, making it easier for individuals to focus on breaking the habit of smoking. NRT can also be used in combination with other smoking cessation strategies, such as counseling or support groups, to increase the likelihood of success in quitting smoking for good.

It's important to note that while NRT can be an effective tool in reducing nicotine dependence, it's not a magic solution. Quitting smoking requires commitment, determination, and a willingness to make lifestyle changes. NRT should be used as part of a comprehensive quit plan that includes setting a quit date, identifying triggers and coping strategies, and seeking support from friends, family, or healthcare professionals.

In addition to using NRT, individuals can also benefit from making positive changes in their daily routine. Engaging in regular physical activity, finding healthy alternatives to smoking, and practicing stress-reducing techniques can all contribute to a successful quit journey. It's essential for individuals to stay motivated and focused on their goal of becoming smoke-free for life.

Ultimately, the decision to use NRT as a method to gradually reduce nicotine dependence is a personal one. It's essential for individuals to educate themselves about the different NRT products available, understand how they work, and consult with a healthcare professional to determine the best approach for their specific needs. With dedication and perseverance, using NRT can be a valuable tool in the journey to becoming smoke-free for life.

Potential side effects and how to manage them

Quitting smoking is a commendable and life-changing decision, but it is not without its challenges. As you embark on this journey towards a smoke-free life, it's important to be aware of the potential side effects that may arise along the way. Understanding these side effects and knowing how to manage them can greatly increase your chances of successfully quitting smoking for good.

One of the most common side effects of quitting smoking is nicotine withdrawal. When you stop smoking, your body goes through a period of adjustment as it craves the nicotine it has become accustomed to. This can lead to symptoms such as irritability, anxiety, restlessness, and difficulty concentrating. To manage these withdrawal symptoms, it can be helpful to use nicotine replacement therapy, such as nicotine gum, patches, or lozenges. These products can help ease the cravings and reduce the severity of withdrawal symptoms.

Another potential side effect of quitting smoking is weight gain. Many people find that they gain a few pounds after they quit smoking, as they may turn to food as a substitute for cigarettes. To manage this side effect, it's important to be mindful of your eating habits and to focus on making healthy food choices. Regular exercise can also help prevent weight gain and improve your overall well-being.

Some people may also experience mood swings and depression as they go through the process of quitting smoking. This can be attributed to the chemical changes that occur in the brain when nicotine is no longer present. To manage these symptoms, it's important to seek support from friends, family, or a support group. Counseling or therapy can also be beneficial in addressing any underlying mental health issues that may arise during the quitting process.

It's also common for people to experience cravings for cigarettes, especially in situations where they used to smoke, such as after a meal or during a break at work. To manage these cravings, it can be helpful to find alternative activities to distract yourself, such as going for a walk, chewing gum, or practicing deep breathing exercises. Developing a plan for how to handle cravings in advance can make it easier to resist the temptation to smoke.

Some people may also experience physical symptoms such as coughing, sore throat, and chest tightness as their body begins to heal from the damage caused by smoking. These symptoms are usually temporary and will improve over time. Drinking plenty of water and using throat lozenges can help soothe a sore throat, while staying physically active can help improve lung function and reduce coughing.

In conclusion, it's important to be aware of the potential side effects of quitting smoking and to have a plan in place for managing them. By understanding these challenges and knowing how to address them, you can increase your chances of successfully quitting smoking and staying smoke-free for life. Remember that everyone's quitting journey is unique, and it's okay to seek support and guidance along the way. Stay committed to your goal of living a smoke-free life, and remember that the benefits of quitting smoking far outweigh any temporary side effects.

Chapter 4: Behavioral Strategies for Quitting

Identifying and changing smoking

Identifying and changing smoking habits is a critical step in the journey toward a smoke-free life. It requires a deep understanding of the triggers and patterns that lead to smoking behavior. By recognizing these triggers and patterns, individuals can begin to make meaningful changes that will support their efforts to quit smoking for good.

One key aspect of identifying and changing smoking habits is understanding the psychological and emotional factors that contribute to the habit. Many individuals use smoking as a means of coping with stress, anxiety, or other difficult emotions. By addressing these underlying issues, individuals can begin to develop healthier coping mechanisms that do not involve smoking. This may involve seeking professional support, such as therapy or counseling, to work through these emotional challenges.

Another important aspect of identifying and changing smoking habits is recognizing the environmental and social triggers that may lead to smoking. For example, being around friends or family members who smoke, or spending time in places where smoking is common, can make it more difficult to resist the urge to smoke. By identifying these triggers, individuals can begin to make changes in their social and environmental surroundings that will support their efforts to quit smoking.

Once individuals have identified the triggers and patterns that contribute to their smoking habits, they can begin to make changes that will support their efforts to quit. This may involve making changes to their daily routines, finding new, healthier ways to cope with stress and difficult emotions, or seeking out new social environments that are more supportive of their goal to quit smoking.

It's important to approach the process of identifying and changing smoking habits with patience and self-compassion. Changing deeply ingrained habits is not easy, and it may take time to see progress. By being kind and patient with oneself, individuals can create an environment that is supportive of their efforts to quit smoking for good.

In conclusion, identifying and changing smoking habits is a crucial step in the journey toward a smoke-free life. By understanding the psychological, emotional, environmental, and social factors that contribute to smoking, individuals can begin to make meaningful changes that will support their efforts to quit smoking for good. By approaching this process with patience and self-compassion, individuals can create an environment that is supportive of their goal to live a smoke-free life.

Coping mechanisms for stress and anxiety

Coping mechanisms for stress and anxiety are crucial for individuals who are trying to quit smoking. The urge to smoke is often triggered by stress and anxiety, so having effective strategies in place to manage these emotions is essential for long-term success. One of the most important coping mechanisms is the ability to recognize and acknowledge stress and anxiety when they arise. This self-awareness allows individuals to take proactive steps to address these emotions before they escalate and lead to a relapse.

One effective coping mechanism is mindfulness meditation, which has been shown to reduce stress and anxiety levels. By practicing mindfulness, individuals can learn to observe their thoughts and feelings without judgment, which can help them to respond to stressful situations in a more calm and composed manner. Another useful strategy is deep breathing exercises, which can help to activate the body's relaxation response and reduce feelings of tension and anxiety.

Engaging in regular physical activity is another effective coping mechanism for stress and anxiety. Exercise releases endorphins, which are natural mood lifters, and can also help individuals to manage their weight, improve their overall health, and reduce their risk of developing smoking-related illnesses. Additionally, engaging in enjoyable activities and hobbies can provide a much-needed distraction from stress and anxiety, and can help individuals to relax and unwind.

Social support is also an important coping mechanism for stress and anxiety. Having a strong support network of friends, family, and peers who are also committed to quitting smoking can provide individuals with encouragement, understanding, and accountability. This support can help individuals to feel less isolated and more motivated to stay smoke-free.

Finally, developing healthy coping mechanisms for stress and anxiety often involves making positive lifestyle changes. This can include getting an adequate amount of sleep each night, eating a balanced diet, and avoiding excessive consumption of caffeine and alcohol, all of which can contribute to feelings of stress and anxiety. It's also important for individuals to practice self-care and prioritize their own well-being, whether it's through engaging in regular relaxation techniques, such as yoga or spending time in nature.

In conclusion, coping mechanisms for stress and anxiety are essential for individuals who are striving to quit smoking. By developing effective strategies to manage these emotions, individuals can increase their chances of long-term success in their smoke-free journey. Whether it's through mindfulness meditation, physical activity, social support, or positive lifestyle changes, finding healthy ways to cope with stress and anxiety can help individuals to stay committed to their goal of becoming smoke-free for life.

Creating new routines and activities to replace smoking

Quitting smoking is not just about giving up a bad habit, it's also about creating new routines and activities to replace the act of smoking. For many people, smoking is not just a physical addiction, but also a deeply ingrained habit that is associated with various activities and routines throughout the day. When you decide to quit smoking, it's important to identify these triggers and find alternative activities to replace them.

One of the first steps in creating new routines and activities is to identify the times and situations when you are most likely to crave a cigarette. This could be after a meal, during your work break, or when you are feeling stressed. Once you have identified these triggers, you can then come up with alternative activities to replace smoking during these times. For example, instead of reaching for a cigarette after a meal, you could go for a short walk or practice deep breathing exercises to help you relax.

In addition to identifying triggers and finding alternatives, it's also important to incorporate new activities into your daily routine to help distract you from the urge to smoke. This could be anything from taking up a new hobby, such as painting or gardening, to joining a fitness class or sports team. By filling your time with new and enjoyable activities, you can help to break the association between certain activities and smoking, making it easier to stay smoke-free.

It's also important to surround yourself with supportive people who can help you stay on track with your new routines and activities. This could be friends or family members who can provide encouragement and accountability, or it could be joining a support group or online community of people who are also trying to quit smoking. By surrounding yourself with positive influences, you can help to reinforce your new routines and activities and build a strong support system to help you stay smoke-free for life.

In conclusion, creating new routines and activities to replace smoking is an essential part of the quitting process. By identifying triggers, finding alternatives, and incorporating new activities into your daily routine, you can help to break the association between certain activities and smoking, making it easier to stay smoke-free. Additionally, surrounding yourself with supportive people can help to reinforce your new routines and activities and provide the encouragement and accountability you need to stay on track. With dedication and perseverance, you can create a new, smoke-free life for yourself and enjoy all the benefits of a healthier, happier lifestyle.

Using cognitive behavioral techniques to challenge smoking

As a professional copywriter with extensive experience in the field of smoking cessation, I am well-versed in the cognitive behavioral techniques that can be used to challenge smoking behavior. Cognitive behavioral therapy (CBT) is a widely recognized and effective approach for addressing the thoughts, feelings, and behaviors that contribute to smoking addiction.

One of the key principles of CBT is the concept of identifying and challenging negative thought patterns that may lead to smoking. This involves helping individuals become more aware of their automatic thoughts and beliefs about smoking, and then working to reframe or challenge those thoughts in a more constructive and realistic way.

For example, if a person has a belief that smoking helps them cope with stress, a CBT therapist might work with them to identify alternative coping strategies that are healthier and more effective in the long run. This could involve teaching the individual relaxation techniques, stress management skills, and other coping mechanisms to replace the perceived benefits of smoking.

Another important component of using cognitive behavioral techniques to challenge smoking is the process of identifying and modifying triggers that may lead to smoking behavior. By helping individuals become more aware of the situations, emotions, or environmental cues that prompt them to smoke, CBT can empower them to develop alternative responses to these triggers.

This might involve practicing mindfulness techniques to become more present and aware of their internal and external triggers, as well as developing strategies for managing cravings and urges to smoke. By learning to recognize and respond to these triggers in a healthier way, individuals can gradually reduce their reliance on smoking as a coping mechanism.

In addition to addressing negative thought patterns and triggers, CBT also emphasizes the importance of developing and practicing new, healthier behaviors to replace smoking. This could involve setting specific goals for behavior change, such as increasing physical activity, improving nutrition, or engaging in activities that provide a sense of fulfillment and satisfaction.

By focusing on the development of new behaviors and habits, individuals can gradually shift their focus away from smoking and towards more positive and rewarding activities. This can help to disrupt the cycle of smoking behavior and create a pathway towards long-term abstinence.

Overall, the use of cognitive behavioral techniques to challenge smoking is a powerful and evidence-based approach for helping individuals break free from the grip of smoking addiction. By addressing negative thought patterns, modifying triggers, and developing new behaviors, CBT can empower individuals to take control of their smoking behavior and move towards a smoke-free life.

In my experience as a copywriter and author in the field of smoking cessation, I have seen firsthand the transformative power of cognitive behavioral techniques in helping individuals quit smoking and stay quit. By providing practical strategies and tools for challenging smoking behavior, CBT can offer a roadmap for lasting change and a healthier, smoke-free future.

Chapter 5: Overcoming Withdrawal Symptoms

Understanding common withdrawal symptoms

Quitting smoking is a commendable decision, but it can come with its own set of challenges. One of the most common hurdles that individuals face when they decide to quit smoking is dealing with withdrawal symptoms. Understanding these symptoms is crucial for anyone who is serious about quitting smoking for good.

Withdrawal symptoms are the body's way of reacting to the absence of nicotine, the addictive substance found in cigarettes. These symptoms can vary from person to person, but some of the most common ones include irritability, anxiety, restlessness, and difficulty concentrating. Many individuals also experience physical symptoms such as headaches, increased appetite, and insomnia.

It's important to remember that these symptoms are only temporary and will eventually subside as the body adjusts to being smoke-free. However, it's still important to have a plan in place to deal with these symptoms when they arise. One effective strategy is to find healthy ways to cope with stress, such as exercise, meditation, or deep breathing exercises. It's also helpful to have a support system in place, whether it's friends, family members, or a support group. Having someone to talk to when cravings or withdrawal symptoms hit can make a world of difference.

Another common withdrawal symptom is the intense craving for nicotine. These cravings can be incredibly powerful and can make it difficult to stay committed to quitting. However, it's important to remember that these cravings are only temporary and will become less intense over time. Finding healthy distractions, such as engaging in a hobby or going for a walk, can help to take your mind off the craving and reduce its intensity.

Physical symptoms such as headaches and increased appetite can also be challenging to deal with. Staying hydrated and eating healthy, balanced meals can help to alleviate some of these symptoms. Engaging in regular physical activity can also help to reduce the intensity of these symptoms and improve overall well-being.

Understanding these common withdrawal symptoms and having a plan in place to deal with them is crucial for anyone who is serious about quitting smoking for good. While these symptoms can be challenging, they are only temporary and will eventually subside. By finding healthy ways to cope with these symptoms and having a support system in place, individuals can increase their chances of successfully quitting smoking and staying smoke-free for life.

Strategies for managing physical and psychological discomfort

As you embark on your journey to become smoke-free for life, it's important to be prepared for the physical and psychological discomfort that may arise as you work towards quitting smoking and staying quit. Managing these challenges effectively is crucial to your success in breaking free from the grip of nicotine addiction.

One of the key strategies for managing physical discomfort is to stay active. Engaging in regular physical activity can help alleviate withdrawal symptoms and reduce the urge to smoke. Exercise also releases endorphins, which can improve your mood and help you cope with stress and anxiety. Additionally, staying hydrated and eating a balanced diet can support your body's natural detoxification process and minimize the physical discomfort associated with nicotine withdrawal.

In addition to physical discomfort, many individuals also experience psychological challenges when trying to quit smoking. It's important to develop coping mechanisms to address these issues. One effective strategy is to practice mindfulness and relaxation techniques. Mindfulness can help you stay present and focused, reducing the impact of cravings and negative emotions. Deep breathing exercises, meditation, and progressive muscle relaxation are all effective techniques for managing psychological discomfort.

Another valuable strategy for managing psychological discomfort is to seek support from others. Connecting with friends, family, or support groups can provide you with the encouragement and understanding you need to navigate the emotional ups and downs of quitting smoking. Talking to a therapist or counselor can also be beneficial, as they can offer professional guidance and support as you work through the psychological challenges of quitting.

It's also important to develop healthy habits and routines to replace the act of smoking. Engaging in activities that bring you joy and fulfillment can help fill the void left by smoking and reduce feelings of discomfort. Whether it's pursuing a hobby, spending time in nature, or practicing self-care, finding alternative sources of pleasure and relaxation can make the transition to a smoke-free life more manageable.

Finally, it's crucial to stay positive and motivated throughout your journey. Remind yourself of the reasons why you want to quit smoking and focus on the benefits of a smoke-free life. Celebrate your progress and small victories along the way, and be kind to yourself during moments of struggle. Maintaining a positive mindset and a sense of determination can help you push through discomfort and stay committed to your goal of becoming smoke-free for life.

In conclusion, managing physical and psychological discomfort is an essential part of the journey to quit smoking and stay quit. By implementing strategies such as staying active, practicing mindfulness, seeking support, developing healthy habits, and maintaining a positive mindset, you can effectively navigate the challenges that arise and ultimately achieve success in your quest for a smoke-free life. Remember, you have the strength and resilience to overcome discomfort and create a healthier, happier future for yourself.

The timeline for withdrawal and when symptoms are most severe

Quitting smoking is a significant step towards better health and well-being. However, it's important to understand that the process of withdrawal can be challenging. The timeline for withdrawal and when symptoms are most severe can vary from person to person, but there are general patterns that many people experience.

In the first few hours after quitting, you may start to feel the onset of withdrawal symptoms. These can include feelings of irritability, anxiety, and intense cravings for a cigarette. As the first day progresses, these symptoms may intensify, making it crucial to have a plan in place to manage them.

By the second and third day, the physical symptoms of withdrawal, such as headaches, nausea, and increased appetite, may become more pronounced. This is when many people find it most challenging to stay smoke-free, as the body is still adjusting to the absence of nicotine.

The first week is often the most difficult, as the body continues to detoxify from the effects of smoking. You may experience mood swings, difficulty concentrating, and intense cravings. It's important to stay focused on your reasons for quitting and to seek support from friends, family, or a support group.

By the second and third week, the physical symptoms of withdrawal typically begin to subside. However, psychological cravings and triggers may still be present. It's important to remain vigilant and continue to utilize coping strategies to prevent relapse.

As you approach the one-month mark, the frequency and intensity of cravings should continue to decrease. At this point, many people start to feel a renewed sense of energy and well-being, as the body continues to heal from the damage caused by smoking.

By the three-month mark, most physical withdrawal symptoms should be resolved. However, it's important to remain vigilant, as psychological triggers and cravings can still emerge. It's essential to continue utilizing coping strategies and seeking support to maintain your smoke-free status.

At six months, many people find that the urge to smoke has significantly diminished. The health benefits of quitting smoking, such as improved lung function and reduced risk of heart disease, become more apparent. It's important to celebrate your success and continue to prioritize your health.

By the one-year mark, many people feel confident in their ability to remain smoke-free. However, it's important to remain mindful of potential triggers and to continue utilizing support systems. It's also important to recognize and celebrate the significant achievement of being smoke-free for a year.

In conclusion, the timeline for withdrawal and when symptoms are most severe can vary from person to person. However, understanding the general patterns of withdrawal can help you prepare for the challenges ahead and remain committed to your goal of being smoke-free for life. Remember that you are not alone in this journey, and seeking support from others can make all the difference in successfully quitting smoking and staying quit.

The importance of staying motivated during this challenging period

Quitting smoking is a challenging endeavor. It requires a great deal of motivation and determination to overcome the cravings and withdrawal symptoms that come with breaking the habit. Staying motivated during this period is crucial to your success in becoming smoke-free for life. It's important to keep your eye on the prize and remind yourself of the numerous benefits of quitting smoking.

One of the most effective ways to stay motivated is to set clear and achievable goals for yourself. Whether it's a short-term goal of making it through the day without a cigarette or a long-term goal of improving your overall health, having something to work towards can help keep you focused and motivated. Additionally, surrounding yourself with a strong support system can make a world of difference. Whether it's friends, family, or a support group, having people in your corner who can offer encouragement and accountability can be incredibly helpful.

Another important aspect of staying motivated is to find healthy ways to cope with stress and manage your emotions. Many people turn to smoking as a way to deal with stress, so it's crucial to find alternative methods for managing your emotions that don't involve reaching for a cigarette. Whether it's exercise, meditation, or spending time with loved ones, finding healthy outlets for stress can help keep you on track with your quit journey.

It's also important to celebrate your successes along the way. Quitting smoking is no small feat, and every milestone you reach should be acknowledged and celebrated. Whether it's making it through the first week without a cigarette or hitting the one-year mark, taking the time to recognize and reward yourself for your progress can help keep you motivated to continue on your smoke-free journey.

Lastly, it's essential to stay educated and informed about the dangers of smoking and the benefits of quitting. Reminding yourself of the negative impact smoking has on your health, as well as the positive changes you can experience by quitting, can serve as a powerful motivator to stay on track. Additionally, staying informed about the resources and support available to you can help keep you motivated and engaged in your quit journey.

In conclusion, staying motivated during the challenging period of quitting smoking is essential to your success. Setting clear goals, building a strong support system, finding healthy ways to cope with stress, celebrating your successes, and staying informed about the benefits of quitting can all help keep you motivated and on track to becoming smoke-free for life. Remember, quitting smoking is a journey, and staying motivated is key to reaching your destination.

Chapter 6: Building a Smoke-Free Lifestyle

Finding healthy alternatives to smoking

As a professional copywriter with extensive experience in the field of smoking cessation, I understand the importance of finding healthy alternatives to smoking. While quitting smoking can be a challenging journey, it is essential to explore alternative options that can help individuals stay smoke-free for life.

One of the most effective alternatives to smoking is engaging in physical activity. Exercise not only helps distract individuals from the urge to smoke but also provides a natural way to reduce stress and improve overall well-being. Whether it's going for a brisk walk, practicing yoga, or hitting the gym, finding an activity that is enjoyable and fulfilling can make a significant difference in the quitting process.

Another healthy alternative to smoking is adopting a nutritious diet. Consuming a variety of fruits, vegetables, and whole grains can help combat cravings and provide essential nutrients that support the body's healing process. Additionally, staying hydrated by drinking plenty of water can help flush out toxins and keep the body functioning optimally.

Engaging in mindfulness and relaxation techniques can also serve as healthy alternatives to smoking. Practices such as meditation, deep breathing exercises, and progressive muscle relaxation can help individuals manage stress and reduce the desire to smoke. These techniques promote a sense of calm and focus, making it easier to resist the temptation to reach for a cigarette.

For those who enjoy the act of smoking itself, exploring alternatives such as herbal cigarettes or nicotine replacement therapy can be beneficial. Herbal cigarettes provide a similar smoking experience without the harmful effects of tobacco, while nicotine replacement therapy, such as patches or gum, can help manage withdrawal symptoms and cravings.

In addition to these alternatives, finding a support system can be crucial in maintaining a smoke-free lifestyle. Connecting with others who are also on the journey to quit smoking can provide encouragement, accountability, and valuable tips for staying smoke-free.

Ultimately, finding healthy alternatives to smoking is a personalized journey that requires experimentation and perseverance. By exploring different options and finding what works best for each individual, it is possible to overcome the addiction to smoking and lead a healthier, smoke-free life.

Embracing physical activity and exercise

Physical activity and exercise play a crucial role in the process of quitting smoking and maintaining a smoke-free lifestyle. Engaging in regular physical activity not only helps to distract you from cravings and withdrawal symptoms, but it also has a positive impact on your overall health and well-being. When you quit smoking, your body goes through a period of adjustment as it begins to heal from the damage caused by years of smoking. Exercise can aid in this process by improving circulation, increasing lung capacity, and reducing the risk of weight gain.

Incorporating physical activity into your daily routine doesn't have to be overwhelming or time-consuming. Even small changes, such as taking the stairs instead of the elevator or going for a brisk walk during your lunch break, can make a significant difference. Finding an activity that you enjoy and look forward to can make it easier to stay committed and motivated. Whether it's cycling, swimming, dancing, or yoga, there are countless options to choose from. The key is to find something that resonates with you and fits into your lifestyle.

Regular exercise not only benefits your physical health but also has a positive impact on your mental and emotional well-being. It can help reduce stress, anxiety, and depression, all of which are common triggers for smoking. Exercise releases endorphins, which are natural mood lifters, and promotes a sense of accomplishment and empowerment. It can also improve your sleep quality, which is essential for managing cravings and staying focused on your goal of remaining smoke-free.

In addition to the immediate benefits, regular physical activity can also help reduce the risk of developing smoking-related illnesses in the long run. It can lower your risk of heart disease, stroke, and certain types of cancer, all of which are heightened for smokers. By investing in your physical health through exercise, you are not only improving your quality of life but also increasing your chances of staying smoke-free for the long haul.

When incorporating physical activity into your smoke-free lifestyle, it's important to set realistic goals and gradually build up your level of activity. Start with small, achievable targets and gradually increase the intensity and duration of your workouts as your fitness improves. It's also important to listen to your body and give yourself time to rest and recover. Overexerting yourself can lead to burnout and increase the risk of relapse.

In conclusion, embracing physical activity and exercise is an integral part of the journey to becoming smoke-free for life. It offers a wide range of physical, mental, and emotional benefits that can support you through the challenges of quitting smoking and help you maintain a healthy, smoke-free lifestyle in the long term. By making physical activity a priority and finding activities that you enjoy, you can enhance your overall well-being and increase your chances of success in your journey to quit smoking for good.

Rebuilding social connections without cigarettes

As a professional copywriter with a wealth of experience in the field of smoking cessation, I understand the importance of rebuilding social connections without relying on cigarettes. The transition from being a smoker to a non-smoker can be challenging, especially when it comes to social situations. Many individuals have formed deep associations between smoking and socializing, making it difficult to navigate social interactions without the crutch of a cigarette. However, it is entirely possible to rebuild social connections without cigarettes and create new, healthier habits that support a smoke-free lifestyle.

One of the first steps in rebuilding social connections without cigarettes is to be open and honest with friends and family about your decision to quit smoking. By communicating your goals and seeking support from your loved ones, you can create a network of individuals who are invested in your success. Surrounding yourself with positive influences and individuals who respect your decision to quit smoking can make a significant difference in your ability to navigate social situations without feeling tempted to pick up a cigarette.

Additionally, finding alternative activities to replace the habit of smoking during social interactions can be incredibly beneficial. Engaging in activities that keep your hands and mind occupied, such as playing a game or participating in a hobby, can help distract you from the urge to smoke. Furthermore, seeking out smoke-free environments and social gatherings can provide a supportive atmosphere that aligns with your smoke-free goals.

Another essential aspect of rebuilding social connections without cigarettes is to reframe your mindset around socializing. Rather than associating social interactions with smoking, focus on the genuine connections and experiences that come from spending time with others. Embracing the opportunity to engage in meaningful conversations, enjoy delicious food, and partake in enjoyable activities can help shift your focus away from the habit of smoking.

It's also crucial to establish new routines and rituals that support your smoke-free lifestyle. Whether it's taking a walk with a friend after a meal or attending a fitness class together, incorporating healthy activities into your social interactions can reinforce your commitment to quitting smoking. By creating new traditions and rituals that do not involve cigarettes, you can cultivate a sense of fulfillment and satisfaction in your social experiences.

In addition to building new social connections, it's essential to nurture existing relationships with individuals who support your smoke-free journey. Surrounding yourself with friends and family members who respect your decision to quit smoking and encourage your progress can provide a strong foundation for navigating social situations without cigarettes. Cultivating these positive connections can help reinforce your commitment to a smoke-free life and provide a sense of camaraderie and support.

Ultimately, rebuilding social connections without cigarettes requires a combination of open communication, alternative activities, mindset shifts, new routines, and supportive relationships. By embracing these strategies, you can navigate social interactions with confidence and determination, knowing that you are capable of creating meaningful connections without the need for cigarettes. It's important to remember that quitting smoking is a journey, and rebuilding social connections is an integral part of that process. With perseverance and the right support, you can successfully transition to a smoke-free life and thrive in social settings without the crutch of cigarettes.

Creating a smoke

Quitting smoking and staying smoke-free is a challenging journey for many individuals. One of the crucial steps in this process is creating a smoke-free environment. This is essential to ensure that temptations and triggers are minimized, making it easier to stay committed to the goal of being smoke-free for life.

First and foremost, it is important to eliminate all smoking paraphernalia from your living space. This includes ashtrays, lighters, and any remaining cigarettes. By removing these items, you are reducing the immediate access to smoking, which can help decrease the urge to smoke. Additionally, cleaning your living space to remove any lingering smoke odors can also contribute to creating a smoke-free environment.

Another important aspect of creating a smoke-free environment is establishing clear boundaries with friends and family who smoke. It may be necessary to communicate your decision to quit smoking and request their support in not smoking around you or offering you cigarettes. Surrounding yourself with individuals who respect and support your commitment to being smoke-free can greatly impact your success in quitting smoking.

In addition to addressing the physical environment, it is also crucial to address the emotional and psychological aspects of creating a smoke-free environment. This may involve identifying and avoiding situations or activities that are strongly associated with smoking. For example, if taking a smoke break during work was a regular habit, finding alternative activities to replace that time can be beneficial. Engaging in physical exercise, practicing mindfulness, or pursuing a new hobby can help fill the void left by smoking and reduce the likelihood of relapse.

Furthermore, it can be helpful to seek out support from a smoking cessation program, counselor, or support group. Surrounding yourself with individuals who are also on the journey to quit smoking can provide a sense of community and understanding. Sharing experiences, challenges, and successes with others can offer valuable encouragement and motivation to stay smoke-free.

Creating a smoke-free environment is not a one-time task, but an ongoing commitment. It requires diligence, perseverance, and a willingness to adapt to new routines and habits. By taking proactive steps to eliminate smoking triggers, communicate boundaries with others, and seek out support, individuals can enhance their chances of successfully quitting smoking and maintaining a smoke-free lifestyle.

In conclusion, creating a smoke-free environment is a fundamental component of the journey to quitting smoking and staying smoke-free for life. By addressing the physical, emotional, and psychological aspects of the environment, individuals can reduce the likelihood of relapse and increase their chances of long-term success. It is imperative to take proactive steps, seek out support, and remain committed to the goal of being smoke-free. With dedication and perseverance, it is possible to create a smoke-free environment and embrace a healthier, smoke-free lifestyle.

Chapter 7: Managing Cravings and Triggers

Identifying and avoiding triggers

Quitting smoking can be a challenging journey, and one of the key aspects of success is identifying and avoiding triggers. Triggers are the people, places, activities, and emotions that make you crave a cigarette. By recognizing these triggers and taking steps to avoid them, you can greatly increase your chances of staying smoke-free for life.

One of the most common triggers for smoking is stress. When you're feeling stressed, it's easy to reach for a cigarette as a way to cope. To avoid this trigger, it's important to find healthy ways to manage stress. This could include practicing relaxation techniques, such as deep breathing or meditation, or engaging in physical activity, like yoga or jogging. By finding alternative ways to manage stress, you can reduce the urge to smoke.

Another common trigger is being around other people who smoke. If you have friends or family members who smoke, it can be difficult to resist the temptation to join them. In these situations, it's important to communicate your goals and boundaries with the people around you. Let them know that you're trying to quit smoking and ask for their support in not smoking around you. You may also need to avoid certain social situations where smoking is prevalent, at least in the early stages of quitting.

Emotional triggers can also be powerful drivers of smoking behavior. Feelings of sadness, loneliness, or boredom can all lead to cravings for a cigarette. It's important to find healthy ways to cope with these emotions, whether it's talking to a friend, engaging in a hobby, or seeking professional help. By addressing the underlying emotions that drive your smoking habit, you can reduce the power of these triggers.

For many people, certain activities or routines can also act as triggers for smoking. For example, if you have a morning coffee ritual that always includes a cigarette, you may need to change that routine to break the association. This could involve switching to a different beverage, or finding a new morning activity to replace the old one. By disrupting the patterns that trigger your smoking habit, you can weaken their hold on you.

In addition to identifying and avoiding triggers, it's also important to have a plan for dealing with cravings when they do arise. This could involve having a list of distractions or activities that you can turn to when a craving strikes, or having a support system in place to help you through the tough moments. By being prepared for cravings, you can increase your resilience and reduce the likelihood of slipping back into old habits.

Ultimately, identifying and avoiding triggers is an essential part of the process of quitting smoking and staying smoke-free for life. By addressing the people, places, activities, and emotions that drive your smoking habit, you can create a healthier, smoke-free future for yourself. It may not be easy, but with determination and the right strategies, it is possible to overcome your triggers and live a smoke-free life.

Coping strategies for dealing with cravings

As you embark on your journey to become smoke-free for life, it's important to arm yourself with effective coping strategies for dealing with cravings. Cravings can be intense and overwhelming, but with the right tools and mindset, you can overcome them and stay on the path to a smoke-free life.

One of the most effective coping strategies for dealing with cravings is to distract yourself. Engage in activities that keep your mind and hands busy, such as going for a walk, practicing deep breathing exercises, or engaging in a hobby or activity that you enjoy. By redirecting your focus, you can diminish the intensity of the craving and help it pass more quickly.

Another powerful coping strategy is to practice mindfulness and self-awareness. When a craving hits, take a moment to acknowledge it without judgment. Recognize the physical sensations and thoughts that accompany the craving, and remind yourself that it is temporary. By observing the craving without giving in to it, you can gain a sense of control and empowerment over it.

It's also important to have a support system in place. Surround yourself with friends, family, or a support group who understand your goal to quit smoking and can offer encouragement and understanding during challenging times. Having someone to talk to or lean on can make a world of difference when dealing with cravings.

In addition, incorporating healthy lifestyle habits can help diminish the intensity and frequency of cravings. Ensure you are eating a balanced diet, getting regular exercise, and managing stress effectively. These habits can help regulate your body's natural rhythms and reduce the likelihood of experiencing intense cravings.

Furthermore, it's crucial to reframe your mindset and focus on the benefits of being smoke-free. Remind yourself of the reasons why you decided to quit smoking in the first place, whether it's for your health, finances, or relationships. Visualize the positive impact of staying smoke-free and use it as motivation to push through cravings.

Lastly, consider seeking professional help if you find yourself struggling to cope with cravings. There are various resources available, such as counseling, support groups, and nicotine replacement therapies, that can provide additional support and guidance as you navigate the challenges of quitting smoking.

In conclusion, coping with cravings is an essential aspect of achieving and maintaining a smoke-free life. By implementing effective coping strategies, building a strong support system, and focusing on the benefits of quitting smoking, you can overcome cravings and stay committed to your goal of becoming smoke-free for life. Remember that cravings are temporary, and with the right mindset and tools, you can successfully navigate through them and emerge stronger on the other side.

Using mindfulness and relaxation techniques to manage stress

Stress is often cited as one of the main reasons why people struggle to quit smoking. The urge to smoke can be triggered by stress, making it incredibly difficult to kick the habit. This is where mindfulness and relaxation techniques come into play. By learning to manage stress effectively, individuals can increase their chances of successfully quitting smoking and staying smoke-free for life.

Mindfulness is the practice of being fully present and aware of one's thoughts, feelings, and bodily sensations. By incorporating mindfulness into their daily routine, individuals can develop a greater sense of control over their emotions and reactions to stress. This can help them to resist the urge to smoke when faced with challenging situations. One of the key principles of mindfulness is acceptance – accepting one's thoughts and feelings without judgment. This can be particularly beneficial for those trying to quit smoking, as it can help them to acknowledge their cravings without giving in to them.

Relaxation techniques, such as deep breathing, progressive muscle relaxation, and guided imagery, can also be effective in managing stress. These techniques work by activating the body's relaxation response, which counteracts the stress response. By practicing these techniques regularly, individuals can reduce their overall stress levels and decrease their reliance on smoking as a coping mechanism.

Incorporating mindfulness and relaxation techniques into a comprehensive smoking cessation plan can greatly increase the chances of success. In fact, research has shown that mindfulness-based interventions can lead to significant reductions in smoking behavior and cravings. By learning to manage stress in a healthy and effective way, individuals can break free from the cycle of smoking and take control of their lives.

To get started with mindfulness and relaxation, individuals can consider seeking out resources such as guided meditation apps, mindfulness courses, or relaxation CDs. These can provide the guidance and support needed to develop a regular practice. Additionally, finding a quiet and comfortable space to practice mindfulness and relaxation can help to enhance the experience and make it more effective.

It's important to note that mindfulness and relaxation are not quick fixes. They require consistent practice and dedication in order to see results. However, the benefits of incorporating these techniques into a smoking cessation plan can be significant. By learning to manage stress in a healthy and sustainable way, individuals can increase their chances of quitting smoking for good.

In conclusion, mindfulness and relaxation techniques can be powerful tools for managing stress and breaking free from the grip of smoking. By learning to be present in the moment and practicing relaxation exercises, individuals can develop the skills needed to resist the urge to smoke and cope with stress in a healthy way. With dedication and practice, mindfulness and relaxation can be invaluable assets in the journey to becoming smoke-free for life.

The importance of distraction and staying busy during peak craving times

Quitting smoking is a challenging journey, and one of the most difficult aspects is managing cravings, especially during peak craving times. These are the moments when the urge to smoke is at its strongest, and it can feel overwhelming. However, one effective strategy for overcoming these cravings is distraction and staying busy.

The importance of distraction during peak craving times cannot be overstated. When the urge to smoke strikes, finding an activity to occupy your mind and hands can make all the difference. Whether it's taking a brisk walk, doing a crossword puzzle, or simply calling a friend for a chat, engaging in a different activity can help divert your attention away from the craving.

Staying busy is another key component of managing peak cravings. When you're occupied with tasks and activities, there's less mental space available for thoughts of smoking. Consider taking on a new hobby or project to keep yourself engaged and focused. Not only will this help you in the moment, but it can also contribute to a sense of fulfillment and accomplishment as you progress on your smoke-free journey.

It's important to be proactive in identifying activities that work for you during peak craving times. What works for one person may not work for another, so it's essential to experiment and find what helps you personally. Some people find that physical activity, such as exercise or yoga, is particularly effective in managing cravings. Others may find solace in creative pursuits, such as painting or writing. The key is to discover what distracts and engages you in a way that diminishes the power of the craving.

In addition to distraction and staying busy, it's also beneficial to have a support system in place. Whether it's a friend, family member, or support group, having someone to turn to during peak craving times can provide much-needed encouragement and motivation. Sometimes, simply talking through the craving with someone who understands can help lessen its intensity.

Furthermore, practicing mindfulness and relaxation techniques can be valuable tools for managing cravings. Techniques such as deep breathing, meditation, and progressive muscle relaxation can help calm the mind and body, reducing the impact of the craving. By incorporating these practices into your daily routine, you can build resilience against cravings and improve your overall well-being.

It's important to remember that managing cravings is a skill that can be developed over time. It's normal to experience setbacks and challenges along the way, but with persistence and determination, it is possible to overcome even the most intense cravings. By utilizing distraction, staying busy, and leveraging a support system, you can empower yourself to navigate peak craving times with confidence and resilience.

In conclusion, distraction and staying busy during peak craving times are essential strategies for anyone seeking to quit smoking and stay smoke-free for life. By engaging in activities that divert your attention and keep you occupied, you can diminish the power of cravings and strengthen your resolve to remain smoke-free. Combined with a supportive network, mindfulness practices, and a proactive mindset, these strategies can be powerful tools in your journey towards a smoke-free life.

Chapter 8: Staying Quit for the Long-Term

Recognizing and addressing potential relapse triggers

As a seasoned copywriter with extensive knowledge in the field of smoking cessation, I am well-versed in the critical topic of recognizing and addressing potential relapse triggers. In my years of experience, I have come to understand the intricate factors that can lead individuals back to smoking, even after making a firm commitment to quit. It is essential to acknowledge that the journey to becoming smoke-free is not always straightforward, and there are various triggers that can undermine one's efforts to stay quit.

First and foremost, it is crucial to recognize the potential relapse triggers that may arise in daily life. These triggers can manifest in different forms, such as stress, social situations, and emotional distress. It is important to understand that these triggers can vary from person to person, and what may be a significant trigger for one individual may not be as impactful for another. By identifying these triggers, individuals can be better equipped to anticipate and address them effectively.

Once the potential relapse triggers have been identified, it is imperative to develop strategies to address and mitigate them. This may involve implementing coping mechanisms to deal with stress, finding alternative ways to navigate social situations without succumbing to the temptation to smoke, and seeking support to manage emotional distress. Additionally, creating a supportive environment and surrounding oneself with individuals who are understanding of the challenges of quitting smoking can be immensely beneficial in addressing potential relapse triggers.

Furthermore, it is essential to engage in self-reflection and introspection to understand the underlying reasons behind the potential relapse triggers. By gaining insight into the root causes of these triggers, individuals can work towards addressing them at a deeper level, thereby strengthening their resolve to stay smoke-free. This may involve seeking professional help, such as counseling or therapy, to explore and address any underlying psychological or emotional factors that may contribute to the potential relapse triggers.

In addition to addressing the internal factors, it is also important to take proactive steps to modify external triggers in the environment. This may involve making changes to daily routines, avoiding situations or places that may trigger the urge to smoke, and seeking out new, healthy habits to replace the old smoking-related behaviors. By actively modifying the external triggers, individuals can create a supportive environment that reinforces their commitment to staying smoke-free.

In conclusion, recognizing and addressing potential relapse triggers is a critical aspect of the journey to becoming smoke-free for life. By identifying these triggers, developing strategies to address them, engaging in self-reflection, and modifying external triggers, individuals can enhance their ability to stay quit and overcome the challenges that may arise. With the right tools and support, it is possible to navigate the potential relapse triggers and maintain a smoke-free lifestyle for the long term.

Developing a relapse prevention plan

Quitting smoking is an incredible achievement, but the journey doesn't end there. It's important to develop a relapse prevention plan to ensure that you stay smoke-free for life. This plan involves identifying potential triggers and developing strategies to cope with them. One of the first steps in developing a relapse prevention plan is to identify your triggers. These can be anything from stress and social situations to specific times of day or activities. Once you have identified your triggers, it's important to develop strategies to cope with them. This may involve finding alternative ways to deal with stress, avoiding certain social situations, or developing new routines to replace smoking. It's also important to enlist the support of friends, family, or a support group to help you stay on track. Having a strong support system in place can make all the difference when it comes to staying smoke-free. Another key aspect of a relapse prevention plan is to stay mindful of your thoughts and emotions. It's important to recognize when you're experiencing cravings or negative emotions and to have strategies in place to cope with them. This may involve practicing mindfulness or relaxation techniques, engaging in physical activity, or finding healthy distractions. It's also important to have a plan in place in case of a slip-up. If you do have a lapse and smoke a cigarette, it's important not to see it as a failure, but rather as a learning opportunity. Take the time to analyze what led to the lapse and develop strategies to prevent it from happening again in the future. Finally, it's important to celebrate your successes along the way. Staying smoke-free is a huge accomplishment, and it's important to recognize and reward yourself for your hard work. Whether it's treating yourself to something special or simply acknowledging your progress, taking the time to celebrate your achievements can help keep you motivated and focused on staying smoke-free for life. Developing a relapse prevention plan is an essential part of staying smoke-free for life. By identifying your triggers, developing coping strategies, enlisting support, staying mindful, planning for slip-ups, and celebrating your successes, you can set yourself up for long-term success. With dedication and perseverance, you can achieve your goal of living a smoke-free life.

Finding ongoing support and accountability

Quitting smoking is a challenging journey, and finding ongoing support and accountability is crucial for long-term success. Many people struggle to maintain their commitment to a smoke-free lifestyle without the help of a supportive community. Fortunately, there are numerous resources available to provide the necessary support and accountability to help individuals stay on track.

One of the most effective sources of ongoing support is joining a support group or community. These groups offer a safe and non-judgmental space for individuals to share their experiences, struggles, and triumphs with others who are also on the same journey. Being part of a supportive community can provide a sense of belonging and connection, which can be incredibly motivating and empowering.

In addition to support groups, many individuals find ongoing support and accountability through counseling or therapy. Working with a professional can provide personalized guidance and strategies for overcoming triggers and cravings. Therapists can also help individuals address any underlying emotional or psychological factors that may be contributing to their smoking habit.

Another valuable source of ongoing support is enlisting the help of friends and family. Loved ones can offer encouragement, understanding, and accountability to help individuals stay committed to their goal of being smoke-free. Having a strong support system in place can make a significant difference in one's ability to resist the urge to smoke.

Technology has also made it easier than ever to access ongoing support and accountability. There are numerous apps and online communities specifically designed to help individuals quit smoking and stay smoke-free. These resources often provide tools for tracking progress, connecting with others, and accessing helpful tips and information.

In addition to external sources of support, it's important for individuals to cultivate self-accountability. This involves setting clear and realistic goals, developing a plan for managing cravings and triggers, and regularly assessing progress. Self-accountability also involves being honest with oneself about any slip-ups or challenges and taking proactive steps to get back on track.

Ultimately, finding ongoing support and accountability is essential for maintaining a smoke-free lifestyle. Whether it's through support groups, therapy, loved ones, technology, or self-accountability, having the right support system in place can make all the difference in one's ability to quit smoking for good. By seeking out and utilizing these resources, individuals can increase their chances of long-term success and enjoy the many benefits of a smoke-free life.

Celebrating milestones and staying motivated

Quitting smoking is a significant achievement, and it's crucial to celebrate the milestones along the way to staying smoke-free for life. Recognizing and acknowledging your progress is essential for maintaining motivation and staying on track. Whether it's been a week, a month, or a year since you last smoked, each milestone is a reason to celebrate and a reminder of the progress you've made towards a healthier, smoke-free life.

Celebrating milestones can take many forms, from treating yourself to something special to sharing your success with friends and family. It's important to find ways to reward yourself for reaching these milestones, whether it's with a small indulgence or a larger reward for reaching a major milestone. By acknowledging your progress and rewarding yourself for your achievements, you can stay motivated and committed to staying smoke-free.

In addition to celebrating milestones, it's also essential to stay motivated by setting new goals and challenges for yourself. As you reach each milestone, take the time to reflect on your progress and set new targets for the future. Whether it's improving your overall health, saving money, or achieving a personal goal, having something to strive for can help you stay focused and motivated on your journey to staying smoke-free.

Staying connected with others who are also on the path to quitting smoking can also provide motivation and support. Whether it's through a support group, online community, or a trusted friend, having a network of people who understand and support your journey can be incredibly valuable. Sharing your experiences, challenges, and successes with others can help you stay motivated and remind you that you're not alone in your journey to staying smoke-free.

Another way to stay motivated is to focus on the positive changes that come with being smoke-free. From improved health and increased energy to a sense of freedom and empowerment, there are countless benefits to quitting smoking. By focusing on these positive changes, you can stay motivated and committed to maintaining a smoke-free lifestyle. It's important to remind yourself of these benefits regularly and use them as motivation to stay on track.

Finally, staying motivated also means being kind to yourself and recognizing that quitting smoking is a journey with ups and downs. It's normal to experience challenges and setbacks along the way, but it's important to be patient and compassionate with yourself. Instead of being discouraged by setbacks, use them as opportunities to learn and grow, and as motivation to recommit to your goal of staying smoke-free.

In conclusion, celebrating milestones and staying motivated are essential aspects of staying smoke-free for life. By recognizing your progress, rewarding yourself, setting new goals, staying connected with others, focusing on the positive changes, and being compassionate with yourself, you can stay motivated and committed to maintaining a smoke-free lifestyle. Remember that every milestone is a reason to celebrate and a reminder of the progress you've made towards a healthier, smoke-free life.

Chapter 9: The Benefits of Quitting

Improvements to physical health and wellbeing

Quitting smoking can lead to significant improvements in physical health and overall wellbeing. The decision to become smoke-free can have immediate effects on the body, and the long-term benefits are numerous. One of the most noticeable changes is improved lung function. The lungs begin to heal and repair themselves, leading to easier breathing and increased stamina. As a result, physical activities become less strenuous, and overall fitness levels improve. The risk of developing respiratory infections and other lung-related diseases also decreases over time.

Additionally, quitting smoking can have a positive impact on cardiovascular health. The heart and blood vessels begin to repair themselves, reducing the risk of heart disease and stroke. Blood pressure and heart rate may also return to normal levels, further improving cardiovascular function. As a result, the risk of experiencing a heart attack or other cardiovascular-related events decreases over time.

Furthermore, quitting smoking can lead to improvements in overall energy levels. Many people report feeling more energetic and alert after quitting smoking. This can lead to increased productivity and a greater sense of vitality. Improved circulation and oxygenation of the body's tissues also contribute to increased energy levels.

Moreover, quitting smoking can have a positive impact on the body's immune system. The body's ability to fight off infections and illnesses improves over time, leading to a decreased risk of developing colds, flu, and other common ailments. This can result in fewer sick days and an overall improvement in general health.

In addition to physical health benefits, quitting smoking can also lead to improvements in mental and emotional wellbeing. Many people report feeling less stressed and anxious after quitting smoking. This can lead to improved mood and a greater sense of overall wellbeing. The mental clarity and focus that come with quitting smoking can also lead to improved cognitive function and a greater sense of mental sharpness.

Moreover, quitting smoking can lead to improvements in oral health. The risk of developing gum disease and tooth decay decreases over time, leading to improved oral hygiene and overall dental health. This can result in a brighter smile and improved self-confidence.

In conclusion, quitting smoking can lead to numerous improvements in physical health and overall wellbeing. From improved lung function and cardiovascular health to increased energy levels and a stronger immune system, the benefits of becoming smoke-free are numerous and far-reaching. Additionally, the positive impact on mental and emotional wellbeing, as well as oral health, further highlight the importance of quitting smoking for a healthier, happier life. If you are ready to improve your physical health and overall wellbeing, quitting smoking is a crucial first step. With the right support and guidance, you can become smoke-free for life and experience the many benefits that come with it.

The financial savings from quitting smoking

Quitting smoking is not only beneficial for your health, but it also has a significant impact on your finances. The financial savings from quitting smoking can be substantial and can have a positive effect on your overall financial well-being. When you quit smoking, you no longer have to spend money on cigarettes, which can add up to a significant amount over time. In addition to the cost of cigarettes, there are also other financial savings to consider, such as lower health insurance premiums and reduced medical expenses.

The cost of smoking can be quite staggering when you break it down. The average cost of a pack of cigarettes can range from $5 to $15, depending on where you live. If you smoke a pack a day, that can add up to hundreds of dollars a month, and thousands of dollars a year. When you quit smoking, you can save all of that money and put it towards other things, such as paying off debt, saving for a vacation, or investing for the future.

In addition to the direct cost of cigarettes, there are also other financial benefits to quitting smoking. For example, many health insurance companies charge higher premiums for smokers, so when you quit smoking, you may be able to lower your health insurance costs. In addition, smoking is a leading cause of many serious health conditions, such as heart disease, lung cancer, and respiratory issues. By quitting smoking, you can reduce your risk of developing these conditions, which can result in lower medical expenses over the long term.

When you quit smoking, you not only save money, but you also improve your overall financial well-being. You can use the money that you would have spent on cigarettes to pay off debt, save for the future, or invest in your retirement. In addition, you can also save money on health care costs by reducing your risk of developing smoking-related illnesses. This can have a significant impact on your long-term financial security and can help you achieve your financial goals more quickly.

The financial savings from quitting smoking are not just limited to the immediate cost of cigarettes. When you quit smoking, you can also save money on other related expenses, such as dry cleaning and dental care. Smoking can cause your clothes to smell like smoke, which may require more frequent dry cleaning. In addition, smoking can also have a negative impact on your oral health, which can result in higher dental expenses over time. By quitting smoking, you can eliminate these expenses and put that money towards other things that are more important to you.

In conclusion, quitting smoking can have a significant impact on your finances. The financial savings from quitting smoking can be substantial and can have a positive effect on your overall financial well-being. By quitting smoking, you can save money on the cost of cigarettes, lower your health insurance premiums, reduce your risk of developing smoking-related illnesses, and save money on other related expenses. This can help you achieve your financial goals more quickly and improve your long-term financial security. So, if you're looking to improve your financial well-being, quitting smoking may be one of the best investments you can make.

How quitting impacts relationships and social connections

Quitting smoking has a profound impact on relationships and social connections. The decision to quit can lead to a range of reactions from those around you, from support and encouragement to skepticism and doubt. It's important to understand that your decision to quit smoking may change the dynamics of your relationships, both with friends and family. Some people in your life may feel threatened by your decision to quit, especially if they are still smokers. They may see your decision as a reflection of their own habits, and may feel defensive or even resentful. On the other hand, many people will be supportive and proud of your decision to quit, and will offer you encouragement and praise for taking control of your health.

In relationships, quitting smoking can also impact the way you interact with your partner. If your partner is a smoker, they may feel pressured to quit as well, and may struggle with feelings of guilt or inadequacy if they are unable to do so. It's important to communicate openly and honestly with your partner about your decision to quit, and to be supportive of their efforts to quit if they choose to do so. Quitting smoking as a couple can be a powerful bonding experience, and can strengthen your relationship as you work together to overcome the challenges of quitting.

Social connections can also be affected by your decision to quit smoking. Many social activities and gatherings are centered around smoking, and you may find that you need to make adjustments to your social life in order to avoid situations where you may be tempted to smoke. This can be a difficult adjustment, but it's important to remember that your health and well-being are the most important priorities. Over time, you may find that your social connections shift as you seek out activities and friendships that support your smoke-free lifestyle.

Quitting smoking can also change the way you relate to yourself. As you become smoke-free, you may experience a renewed sense of confidence and self-worth. This can have a positive impact on all of your relationships, as you begin to prioritize your own health and well-being. You may find that you have more energy and enthusiasm for social activities, and that you are better able to connect with others in a meaningful and authentic way.

In conclusion, quitting smoking can have a significant impact on relationships and social connections. It's important to be aware of the potential challenges and to communicate openly and honestly with those around you. By prioritizing your health and well-being, you can create stronger, more fulfilling relationships and social connections that support your smoke-free lifestyle.

The positive impact on mental health and emotional wellbeing

Quitting smoking can have a profound and positive impact on your mental health and emotional wellbeing. Many smokers are unaware of the significant influence that smoking has on their mental state and emotional balance. The addictive nature of nicotine can lead to increased anxiety, depression, and mood swings. When you quit smoking, you break free from the cycle of dependence and experience a renewed sense of mental clarity and emotional stability.

One of the most noticeable benefits of quitting smoking is the improvement in mood. Nicotine withdrawal can initially cause irritability and restlessness, but as your body adjusts to being smoke-free, you will likely experience a more balanced and positive mood. Many ex-smokers report feeling less stressed and more emotionally resilient after quitting. This is due in part to the fact that nicotine itself is a stimulant, which can exacerbate feelings of anxiety and agitation.

Furthermore, quitting smoking can lead to better mental focus and concentration. Nicotine addiction can impair cognitive function, making it difficult to concentrate and think clearly. When you quit smoking, you give your brain the opportunity to heal and regain its full capacity. As a result, many ex-smokers find that they are able to think more clearly and perform better in their daily tasks.

In addition to the immediate mental benefits, quitting smoking can also have a long-term positive impact on your emotional wellbeing. Many ex-smokers report feeling a sense of empowerment and control over their lives after quitting. This newfound confidence can have a ripple effect on other areas of your life, leading to improved self-esteem and a more positive outlook on the future.

Moreover, quitting smoking can improve your overall quality of life. Smoking is often a coping mechanism for dealing with stress and negative emotions. However, the temporary relief that smoking provides is outweighed by the long-term negative impact on mental health. By quitting smoking, you can develop healthier coping strategies and learn to manage stress in a more constructive way. This can lead to a greater sense of emotional wellbeing and an overall improvement in mental health.

It's important to note that the positive impact on mental health and emotional wellbeing is not limited to the individual who quits smoking. Research has shown that secondhand smoke exposure can have detrimental effects on the mental health of those around you. By quitting smoking, you not only improve your own mental wellbeing but also create a healthier environment for those close to you.

In conclusion, the decision to quit smoking can have a profound and positive impact on your mental health and emotional wellbeing. From improved mood and concentration to a greater sense of empowerment and control, the benefits of quitting smoking extend far beyond just physical health. If you are ready to take control of your mental and emotional wellbeing, consider taking the first step towards a smoke-free life.

Chapter 10: Helping Others Quit

Supporting friends and family members in their quit journey

Supporting friends and family members in their quit journey is crucial for their success in becoming smoke-free for life. As a professional copywriter with extensive experience in this field, I have seen firsthand the impact that a strong support system can have on someone trying to quit smoking. It is important to approach the situation with empathy and understanding, as quitting smoking is a challenging and often emotional process.

One of the most effective ways to support a friend or family member in their quit journey is to be a good listener. It is essential to create a safe and non-judgmental environment where they feel comfortable expressing their thoughts and feelings about quitting smoking. Encouraging open and honest communication can help them process their emotions and work through any challenges they may face along the way.

In addition to being a good listener, it is important to offer practical support as well. This can include helping them find resources such as support groups, counseling services, or quit smoking programs. You can also assist them in creating a plan for managing cravings and coping with triggers. Offering to participate in activities that distract them from the urge to smoke can also be beneficial.

Furthermore, providing emotional support is crucial in helping a friend or family member stay committed to their quit journey. This can involve offering words of encouragement, celebrating their milestones, and reminding them of the positive impact that quitting smoking will have on their health and well-being. It is also important to be patient and understanding, as there may be setbacks along the way.

It is important to remember that everyone's quit journey is unique, and the support they need may vary. It is essential to respect their individual needs and preferences, and to offer support that is tailored to their specific situation. By being patient, empathetic, and understanding, you can play a significant role in helping your loved ones become smoke-free for life.

Understanding the role of encouragement and non

Encouragement and support play a crucial role in the journey towards becoming smoke-free for life. Understanding the impact of encouragement and non-encouragement can make a significant difference in the success of quitting smoking and staying quit. Encouragement can come in various forms, including verbal praise, emotional support, and practical assistance. It can motivate individuals to stay committed to their goal of living a smoke-free life. On the other hand, non-encouragement, such as criticism or lack of support, can hinder progress and make it more challenging to overcome the addiction to smoking.

When individuals receive encouragement from their loved ones, friends, or support groups, they feel valued and motivated to continue their efforts to quit smoking. Positive reinforcement can boost their confidence and self-esteem, making it easier for them to resist the temptation to smoke. This type of support can also provide a sense of accountability, as individuals are more likely to stay committed to their goal when they know that others believe in their ability to quit smoking. Encouragement can create a positive environment that fosters determination and resilience, essential qualities for overcoming the challenges of quitting smoking.

Conversely, non-encouragement can have detrimental effects on an individual's journey to quit smoking. Criticism or lack of support can lead to feelings of inadequacy and discouragement, making it harder for individuals to stay motivated and focused on their goal. Negative attitudes and comments from others can increase stress and anxiety, which may trigger the urge to smoke as a coping mechanism. This type of non-encouragement can create a barrier to success, as individuals may feel unsupported and misunderstood in their efforts to become smoke-free.

In addition to external sources of encouragement, self-encouragement is also a crucial factor in the process of quitting smoking. Developing a positive mindset and self-belief can empower individuals to overcome the challenges and setbacks they may encounter along the way. Self-encouragement involves acknowledging progress, celebrating small victories, and maintaining a hopeful outlook towards the future. It can help individuals build resilience and determination, which are essential qualities for staying committed to a smoke-free lifestyle.

Understanding the role of encouragement and non-encouragement is vital for individuals who are striving to quit smoking and stay quit. It is essential to surround oneself with a supportive network of individuals who believe in their ability to overcome the addiction to smoking. Encouragement can provide the motivation and strength needed to navigate the ups and downs of the quitting process. It is equally important for individuals to cultivate self-encouragement and maintain a positive mindset, as this can significantly impact their ability to achieve and maintain a smoke-free life.

In conclusion, encouragement and non-encouragement play a crucial role in the journey to becoming smoke-free for life. Positive reinforcement from external sources and self-encouragement can empower individuals to overcome the challenges of quitting smoking and staying quit. Understanding the impact of encouragement and non-encouragement can help individuals build a strong support system and develop the resilience needed to achieve long-term success in living a smoke-free life.

Sharing your own experiences and offering practical assistance

As an experienced copywriter, I understand the importance of sharing personal experiences when it comes to quitting smoking. It's one thing to offer practical advice, but it's another to empathize with others who are going through the same struggle. When you share your own journey of quitting smoking, you can provide valuable insight and inspiration to those who are looking to do the same.

One of the most powerful ways to offer practical assistance is by sharing the specific strategies and techniques that worked for you personally. Whether it's using nicotine replacement therapy, joining a support group, or finding alternative ways to cope with stress, sharing your success stories can give others hope and motivation. Additionally, being transparent about the challenges you faced along the way can help others feel less alone in their own struggles.

In addition to sharing your own experiences, offering practical assistance can also involve providing resources and tools to help others quit smoking. This could include recommending helpful books, apps, or websites, as well as connecting people with local support groups or counseling services. By equipping others with the information and resources they need, you can empower them to take control of their own journey towards a smoke-free life.

Another important aspect of offering practical assistance is being a supportive and non-judgmental presence for those who are trying to quit smoking. It's crucial to listen actively and offer encouragement without imposing your own expectations or timelines. By creating a safe and understanding environment, you can help others feel more comfortable seeking help and staying committed to their goal of quitting smoking.

Ultimately, sharing your own experiences and offering practical assistance is about being a source of inspiration, guidance, and support for those who are on the path to a smoke-free life. By using your own journey as a testament to the possibility of change, you can help others realize that they too can overcome the challenges of quitting smoking. And by providing practical tools and resources, you can empower them to take the necessary steps towards a healthier, smoke-free future.

Resources and organizations that can help others quit smoking

Quitting smoking is a challenging journey, but it's one that is made easier with the support and guidance of resources and organizations dedicated to helping individuals become smoke-free for life. There are numerous options available to those seeking assistance in their quest to quit smoking, and it's important to explore the various resources that exist in order to find the best fit for your needs.

One valuable resource for individuals looking to quit smoking is the American Lung Association. This organization offers a wealth of information and support for those who are trying to kick the habit. From online support groups to in-person cessation programs, the American Lung Association provides a variety of resources to help individuals stay on track and succeed in their efforts to quit smoking.

Another valuable resource for individuals looking to quit smoking is the National Cancer Institute. This organization offers evidence-based smoking cessation resources, including online tools, mobile apps, and publications that can help individuals develop a personalized quit plan and stay motivated throughout their journey to becoming smoke-free for life.

For individuals who prefer a more personalized approach to quitting smoking, seeking out the assistance of a trained smoking cessation counselor or coach can be incredibly beneficial. These professionals are equipped with the knowledge and skills to provide individualized support and guidance to help individuals overcome the challenges of quitting smoking and stay committed to their goal of living smoke-free.

In addition to these national organizations and resources, there are also numerous local and community-based programs and support groups that can provide valuable assistance to individuals looking to quit smoking. These programs often offer a more personalized and localized approach to smoking cessation, and can provide individuals with the opportunity to connect with others who are on a similar journey to becoming smoke-free.

In conclusion, there are a wealth of resources and organizations available to help individuals quit smoking and stay smoke-free for life. Whether you prefer the support of a national organization, the personalized guidance of a smoking cessation counselor, or the community-based approach of a local program, there are options available to suit your individual needs and preferences. By taking advantage of these resources and organizations, you can increase your chances of successfully quitting smoking and enjoying a healthier, smoke-free life.

Don't miss out!

Visit the website below and you can sign up to receive emails whenever Juanita LA publishes a new book. There's no charge and no obligation.

https://books2read.com/r/B-A-WEQOC-XMIDF

BOOKS 2 READ

Connecting independent readers to independent writers.

Did you love *Smoke-Free for Life*? Then you should read *Break the Habit*[1] by Juanita LA!

Breaking the habit of smoking is a challenging but achievable goal that can lead to a healthier and more fulfilling life. As an experienced author and expert in the field, I have dedicated my career to helping individuals overcome their addiction to tobacco and embrace a smoke-free lifestyle. In my best-selling books, I have outlined practical strategies for quitting smoking and living a healthier life, drawing on years of research and personal experience to provide readers with the tools they need to succeed.

Smoking is a pervasive and destructive habit that affects millions of people worldwide. Despite the well-documented health risks and the widespread awareness of the dangers of smoking, many individuals

---

1. https://books2read.com/u/br2Rlw
2. https://books2read.com/u/br2Rlw

struggle to break free from this addictive behavior. The physical and psychological dependence on nicotine, coupled with the social and environmental factors that contribute to smoking, make it a formidable challenge to quit. However, with the right approach and support, it is possible to overcome this addiction and reap the benefits of a smoke-free life.

Also by Juanita LA

Smoke-Free for Life
Break the Habit
Smoke-Free
Clearing the Air
Smoke-Free for Life

Milton Keynes UK
Ingram Content Group UK Ltd.
UKHW042238011124
450424UK00001BA/76